Time-Savers for Teachers

WRITING FICTION YEARS 1-2

W

FRANKLIN WATTS

LONDON•SYDNEY

How to use this book

This book provides a range of worksheets suitable for children in Years 1 and 2 of primary school. The worksheets are grouped into sections which correspond to the text types specified in the National Literacy Strategy. The contents are equally relevant to the Scottish 5–14 Guidelines, and the curricula for the Republic and Northern Ireland.

Each section starts with an introduction. As well as introducing the worksheets, this also details the National Literacy Strategy objectives and suggests approaches to writing. The worksheets have been carefully selected to cater for *different* levels of ability.

At the end of the section, text frames and scaffolds provide guidance for *creative writing* assignments. There are also *assessment sheets* to enable you to keep track of individual children's progress. All teacher-pages have a vertical stripe down the side of the page.

All the worksheets in this book are photocopiable.

This edition first published in 2004

Franklin Watts
96 Leonard Street, London EC2A 4XD

Copyright © in the worksheets Blake Education
Copyright © in this edition Franklin Watts 2004

Contributors: Tanya Dalgleish, Kara Munn, Helen Richards, Lynne Sung, Merryn Whitfield

UK adaptation by Brenda Stones
Educational advisers: Sarah St John, Jo Owston

This edition not for sale outside the United Kingdom and Eire

ISBN 0 7496 5804 5

Printed in Dubai

Contents

NLS Framework

Year 1

<table>
<tr><th></th><th>TERM 1</th><th>TERM 2</th><th>TERM 3</th></tr>
<tr><td rowspan="2">Fiction and poetry</td><td>•stories with familiar settings

•stories and rhymes with predictable and repetitive patterns</td><td>•traditional stories and rhymes

•fairy stories

•stories and poems with familiar, predictable and patterned language from a range of cultures, including playground chants, action verses and rhymes

•plays</td><td>•stories about fantasy worlds

•poems with patterned and predictable structures

•a variety of poems on similar themes</td></tr>
</table>

Year 2

<table>
<tr><th></th><th>TERM 1</th><th>TERM 2</th><th>TERM 3</th></tr>
<tr><td rowspan="2">Fiction and poetry</td><td>•stories and a variety of poems with familiar settings</td><td>•traditional stories: stories and poems from other cultures

•stories and poems with predictable and patterned language

•poems by significant children's poets</td><td>•extended stories

•stories by significant children's authors

•different stories by the same author

•texts with language play, e.g. riddles, tongue-twisters, humorous verse and stories</td></tr>
</table>

4

Introduction to Poetry

NLS objectives

Throughout Years 1 and 2, the reading and writing of poetry should be developed in various ways:

Y1T1 T6: to recite rhymes with predictable and repeating patterns, extemporising on patterns orally by substituting words and phrases, extending patterns, inventing patterns and playing with rhyme;

Y1T1 T10: to use rhymes and patterned stories as models for their own writing;

Y2T1 T12: to use simple poetry structures and to substitute own ideas, write new lines;

Y2T2 T9: to identify and discuss patterns of rhythm, rhyme and other features of sound in different poems.

The worksheets

All the model texts are based either on simple poetic structures or on familiar themes:

Nursery rhymes, with their familiar, predictable and patterned language;

Cinquains, which use a pattern of five lines, here consisting of 1 word, 2 words, 3 words, 4 words, 1 word;

Acrostics, where the initial letter of each line spells out a word linked to the theme of the poem;

Pets and weather, two familiar topics that will enable children to draw on their own observation and experience.

Writing poetry

The simple sample texts, exemplifying the forms above, can act as ideal models for children's own writing.

The simple exercises at the start of the section suggest substituting individual words, or imagining what happens before and after the verse; at the end of the section, frameworks are provided for writing whole new poems.

Humpty Dumpty

Humpty Dumpty sat on a wall,

Humpty Dumpty had a great fall.

All the King's horses
and all the King's men

Couldn't put Humpty together again.

Two nursery rhymes

Hickory Dickory Dock
The mouse ran up the clock.
The clock struck one,
The mouse ran down,
Hickory Dickory Dock.

Jack and Jill
went up the hill
to fetch a pail of water.
Jack fell down
and broke his crown
and Jill came tumbling after.

Before and after

Name _____

1. What do you think happened to make the mouse run up the clock?
Draw your answer in the space below.

Hickory Dickory Dock
The mouse ran up the clock.
The clock struck one,
The mouse ran down,
Hickory Dickory Dock.

2. Draw what you think happened next.

Innovating on a rhyme

Name _____

★ Make up new words to fill the gaps. Make sure the lines still rhyme!

Humpty Dumpty sat on a _____ .

Humpty Dumpty had a _____ _____.

All the King's horses and all the King's men

Couldn't put Humpty together again.

Jack and J_____

went _____ _____ _____

to fetch a pail of water.

Jack _____ _____

and _____ _____ _____

and _____ came tumbling after.

Two nursery rhymes

Jack be nimble
Jack be quick
Jack jump over
the candle stick.

Little Miss Muffet
sat on a tuffet
eating her curds and whey.
Along came a spider
and sat down beside her
and frightened Miss Muffet away.

What did they say?

Name _____

★ Write what you think each character is saying in the speech bubbles.

11

Beginnings and endings

Name _____

★ Match the correct beginnings and endings by colouring in the boxes using the same colour.

Beginnings
Baa Baa
Jack and Jill
Humpty Dumpty
Twinkle twinkle
Hey Diddle Diddle
Mary had a little lamb
Little Miss Muffet
Jack be nimble

Endings
sat on a tuffet
went up the hill
black sheep
sat on a wall
little star
the cat and the fiddle
its fleece was white as snow
Jack be quick

Cinquains

Name _____

★ A cinquain is a poem with five lines.

Teddy
Brown fur
Soft and warm
Sleeps in my bed
Friend

★ How many words are there in each line?

Line 1 _____ Line 2 _____ Line 3 _____

Line 4 _____ Line 5 _____

Food

★ Write a cinquain about something you like to eat.

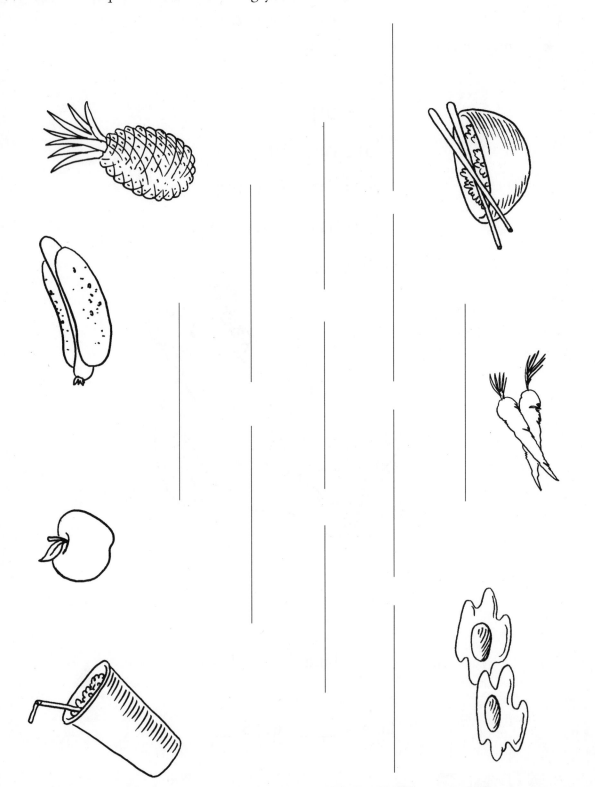

Name _____

★ Write a cinquain about one of your favourite toys.

Acrostics

★ An acrostic is a poem in which one letter of each line spells out a word.

Delicious hamburger
In a fresh bun
Never enough sauce
Nice and juicy
Eat it all up
Really yummy!

★ Read the first letter of each line, going downwards.

What is the word? _____

Let's write

Name _____

★ Write an acrostic poem about one of your friends.

F _____

R _____

I _____

E _____

N _____

D _____

I'm a poet

Name _____

★ Write an acrostic poem using your own name.

Nathan

Mustafa

Blake

Bronson

JACK

Suyin

Ayhan

Sam

Olivia

Miyumi

Josef

Ligi

Koray

Alexandra

My Puppy

I had a little puppy
Fluffy, black and white
With big, black eyes
and a squashy, black nose
I cuddled him every night.

I had a little puppy
With a cheeky little face.
He liked to chew up tissues
and make messes
all over the place.

I had a little puppy
and he grew and
grew some more —
Till I lost that little puppy ...
and now I have a dog.

by Tanya Dalgleish

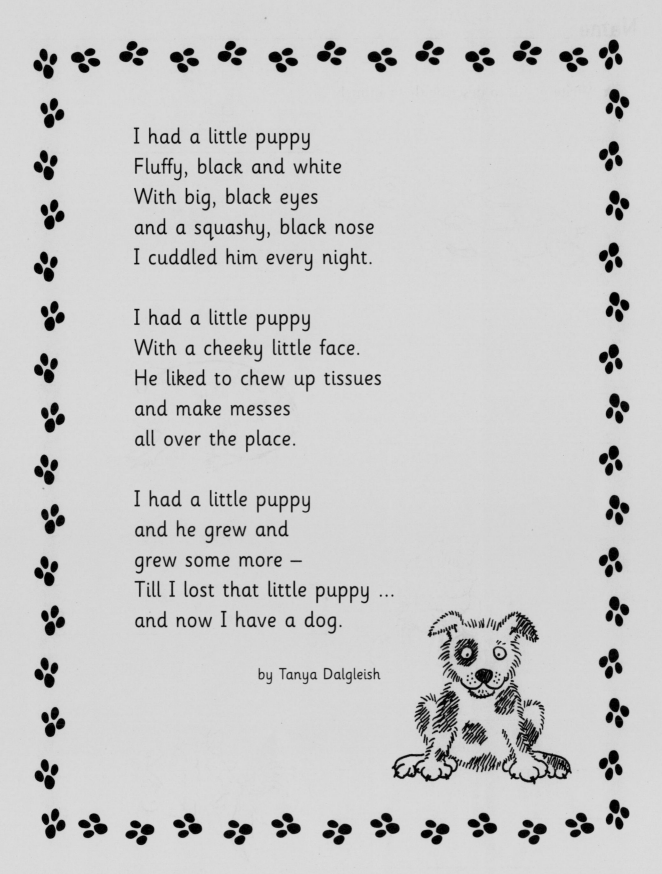

Describing words

Name _____

★ Write words to describe these animals.

_____

_____

_____

_____

_____

_____

_____

_____

_____

_____

_____

_____

_____

_____

_____

Animal noises

Name _____

★ Link each animal with the sound it makes. Draw a line between each match.

yap

miaow

neigh

croak

squeak

chirp

Focus on language

Name _____

1. Write what you think the puppy is saying.

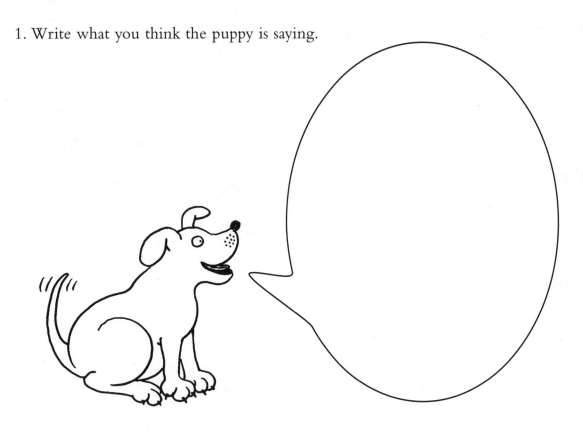

2. Write Yes or No to show whether these sentences are true.

A puppy is a baby cat.   _____

Dogs eat hay.   _____

A baby cow is a calf.   _____

Baby rabbits are called kittens.   _____

Cats eat potatoes.   _____

Focus on language

Name _____

1. Write the sentences correctly on the lines. Remember that sentences start with a capital letter and end with a full stop.

my puppy is black and white

_____

my puppy's name is ben

_____

2. Write plurals for these words. The first one has been done for you.

kitten   kittens_____

nose   _____

eye   _____

face   _____

puppy   _____

3. Circle the words that go with dogs.

kennel	legs	tusks	paws	head
wings	ears	tongue	horns	shell

4. What can a dog do? Circle the verbs (doing words).

jump run lick ears chew growl chase leg nose eyes

Rain

Thunder! Lightning!
Crash! Bang!
Stormy skies
and stones of ice.
Rain pelts down
and drowns the ground.

Storm clouds pass.
Gentle rain
curtains all around.
Pitter pat pitter pat
trickle trickle trickle,
rivulets cross the ground.

Rain stops.
Misty sky and dewy earth
Dampness all around.
Squelch squelch
Splish splosh
Water soaks into the ground.

by Tanya Dalgleish

It's raining

Name _____

★ Write your own rainy day poem on the lines below.

Line 1: What you see

_____

Line 2: What you hear

_____

Line 3: What you smell

_____

Line 4: What you think

_____

Line 5: What you say

_____

★ Share your poem with the rest of your class.

Let's draw!

Name _____

★ Draw yourself on a sunny day.

★ Now write a sunny day poem on another sheet of paper.

Language

Name _____

1. Unjumble the sentences and write them on the lines. Remember to use a capital letter for the beginning of the sentence and a full stop for the end.

(a) the rain down poured

_____

(b) crashed and flashed thunder lightning

_____

(c) soaked the ground up the rain

_____

2. Add punctuation marks, including speech marks, to these sentences.

come out of the rain called mum

rain rain go away chanted Josh

3. Use one of the conjunctions to join the sentences. | and   but   because |

It rained _____ rained all day.

We played inside _____ it was raining.

The sun came out _____ it was still cold.

4. Write an antonym (opposite) for each word.

hot _____, rainy _____, freezing _____

Poetic devices

Name _____

★ Work with a partner and write all the words you can think of that describe the weather.

Words

_____

_____

_____

★ Use some of the words and write a tongue-twister about the weather. Practise saying it really quickly. Teach it to your friends.

Tongue-twister

_____

_____

_____

_____

_____

_____

_____

Be a poet

★ Write a poem about your class.

Look around you at the room, the people, where they are sitting or standing and what they are doing and saying. Now write your poem on the lines below.

Line 1: What you see

_____

Line 2: What you hear

_____

Line 3: What you smell

_____

Line 4: What you think

_____

Line 5: What you say

_____

★ Share your poem with the rest of your class.

From Time-Savers for Teachers: Writing Fiction Years 1-2. This page may be reproduced for classroom use.

29

Poetry writing record

Name _____

Date	Title	Outcomes/ Indicators	Teacher comment	Student evaluation

Summary
Strengths:

Areas for development:

Introduction to Description

NLS objectives

Children should learn to write simple descriptions of objects, places and people before they build up to creating more complex narrative structures:

Y1T3 T8: to compare and contrast stories with a variety of settings, e.g. space, imaginary lands, animal homes;

Y2T2 T14: to write character profiles, e.g. simple descriptions, posters, passports – using key words and phrases that describe or are spoken by characters in the text.

The worksheets

The worksheets progress from describing an object (a real lunch box), to describing a place (the child's own bedroom), and then to describing a person (in this case imaginary).

Even if the objective is to write fictional description, teachers should still encourage children to practise realistic observation of things, places and people, in order to enable them to write convincingly in their eventual narrative.

Writing descriptions

This section breaks down the skills of writing description into brainstorming appropriate nouns, then adjectives and verbs, before planning the overall structure of the descriptive writing.

My Lunch Box

My lunch box is very new. It is made of blue plastic with a yellow flower on the lid. Inside the box there are three spaces.

One space is for my drink bottle, one for a sandwich and one for fruit.

It shuts with a loud snap.

Nobody has a lunch box like mine.

This is my lunch box

★ Have a good look at your lunch box.

Draw and colour it in using the space below. You could draw another picture to show what it looks like inside.

Where is the flower?

★ Cut out the writing below. Put each one under the correct picture.

| on the lid | inside the lid | near the catch |

| behind the writing | underneath the label |

Change the words

Name _____

★ Think of some different words to put in the gaps.

My lunch box

My lunch box is [   ].

It is made of [   ] with a

yellow flower [   ].

Inside the box there are three spaces.

One space is for my drink bottle, one for

a [   ] and one for fruit.

It shuts with [   ].

Nobody has a lunch box like mine.

Guess what's in my lunch box!

Name _____

★ Draw what's inside your lunch box. Can a friend guess what it is?
Then describe it in words.

In my lunch box is a

_____

My magic lunch box

Name _____

★ Imagine that your lunch box is magic. What does it look like? What is inside it? What can it do? Draw and describe your magic lunch box here.

_____

_____

_____

_____

My most marvellous toy

★ Finish the sentences to describe your toy – remember to use full stops!

My Most Marvellous Toy

My most marvellous toy is a _____

_____

It has _____

_____

It looks _____

_____

I keep it _____

_____

I think _____

_____

★ Now draw your toy here.

My Bedroom

My bedroom is at the back of our house.

It has a white door and two large white windows.

The walls are pale blue. My bed is near the window and I can see the tall tree outside in the garden.

The blue and yellow curtains match the bedspread and the cushion on the chair. They have big jungle animals on them.

I keep my teddy on my bed and some books and toys on the bookshelf, but sometimes they fall all over the floor.

There is a big cupboard for my clothes and a little table for my bedside lamp. Above my bed is a colourful, painted picture called The Teddy Bears' Picnic.

I love my bedroom.

What do they look like?

★ If these things belonged to you, what would they look like? Try to think of one or two words to describe each one. Then draw them in the spaces.

bedspread

_____

_____

pyjamas

_____

_____

teddy

_____

_____

toy

_____

_____

picture

_____

_____

chair

_____

_____

outside your window

_____

_____

40

Where are they?

Name _____

★ Where are these things in the bedroom? Draw a line between each match.

the bed   on the chair

the lamp   outside in the garden

the picture   on the bed

teddy   near the window

the tree   above the bed

the cushion   on the little table

What does your bedroom look like?

Name _____

★ Complete these sentences to describe where things are in your bedroom.
Put some drawings in the spaces.

Near the window

_____ .

On the floor

_____ .

Behind my bedroom door

_____ .

Beside my bed

_____ .

Outside the window

_____ .

Track it

★ Look at the words in the box. Choose one to start the second sentence of each pair of sentences. Write it in the gap. Draw a line to connect the pronoun to the noun group it replaces. The first one has been done for you.

It̶	They	He	It	It	They	We

1. (My bedroom) is at the back of the house. (It) has a door and two windows painted white.

2. The car was parked outside the garage door.   was dark blue.

3. We have two friendly dogs.   wait at the gate for us to come home.

4. The curtains match the bedspread and the cushion.   have big jungle animals on them.

5. My teddy stays on my bed.   lies on my pillow.

6. My brother plays in my room.   like to share our toys.

7. The big tree is just outside my window.   shades the whole room.

Draw, tell and listen

Name _____

★ Add some things to this house. You could put in windows, a door, tree, garden, fence, gate, cat, bird or flowers. Then describe your picture to a partner.

Remember to say where each item is, what colour it is and perhaps what shape and what size it is.

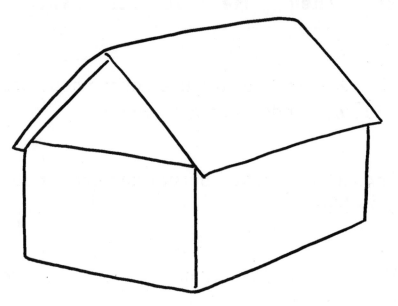

★ Make this house look the way your partner describes it.

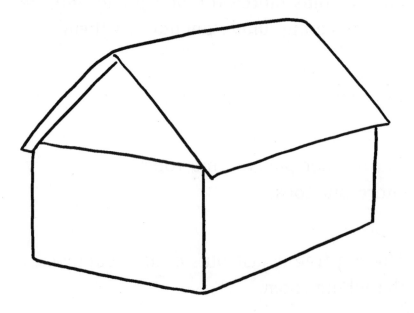

Gordon the Garden Gnome

Gordon stands at the end of the path under the apple tree. His bright red cap seems to twinkle brightly under the dark-green leaves.

It covers his head and hangs down over his back. The blue stripes in his jumper match his long blue trousers which are tucked into his shiny black boots. He carries a spade in one hand and a little bucket of yellow and white daisies in the other.

It is Gordon's face that makes him seem so special. He has fat pink cheeks, a straight nose, beautiful round brown eyes and a dimple in his chin. No-one has heard him, but he always looks as though he is laughing.

There wouldn't be another gnome like Gordon anywhere!

No longer Gordon

Name _____

★ Colour in Gordon and write some words to describe him.

★ Use the bottom of the page to draw another picture, changing the way he looks. Write the changes on the lines. (The first has been done for you.) Give him a new name!

Gordon

_____

_____

_____

_____

a green striped cap

_____

_____

_____

_____

Where's Gordon?

★ Work with a partner. Take turns to find and describe different places for Gordon to stand.

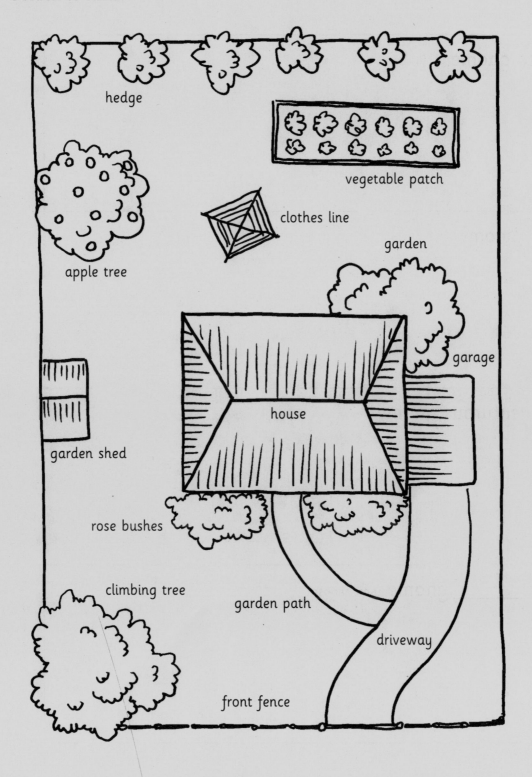

hedge

vegetable patch

clothes line

garden

apple tree

garage

garden shed

house

rose bushes

climbing tree

garden path

driveway

front fence

Name _____

★ Write some words that would help you draw a picture in your mind for each of these gnomes.

a fierce gnome
an old gnome
an adventurous gnome
a _____ gnome (you choose)

Adjective storm

Name _____

★ Choose a garden ornament and draw it in the box. Then think of some words that will help you describe it.

_____

_____

_____

_____

Adjectives

★ Write some adjectives (describing words) to describe your favourite toy.

Planning a description

Name _____

★ Think of something you would like to describe. Draw and write what you want to describe in the box. Then build up some good words around it.

Action verbs

_____

_____

Feeling verbs

_____

_____

Adverbs and adverbial phrases
(how, when, where ...)

_____

_____

Nouns

_____

_____

Adjectives

_____

_____

Description scaffold

Name _____

★ Now plan your own description using the plan below.

Introductory sentence

Descriptive sentence about the subject

Closing comment (optional)

Write your own description

Name _____

★ Now write your own description.

Title

Description

Ending

Description skills checklist

Name:				
Class:	Date/Level	Date/Level	Date/Level	Date/Level
PURPOSE				
Demonstrates understanding of the purpose of descriptions.				
STRUCTURE				
Writes an introductory sentence.				
Develops two or more descriptive features.				
Understands the use of a concluding sentence.				
TEXT ORGANISATION				
Uses text to address a particular subject.				
Develops a plan for writing a description.				
Builds sentences to express clarity and variety.				
Is able to convey objective and subjective ideas.				
LANGUAGE FEATURES				
Uses nouns to build a detailed picture of the subject.				
Uses pronouns to 'track' the subject.				
Makes wide and varied use of adjectives.				
Uses verbs of actions and feelings.				
Writes in the present tense.				
Uses adverbs and adverbial phrases.				
LEVEL CODES 1 Consistently evident	2 Sometimes evident		3 Not evident	

Introduction to Stories

NLS objectives

The progression of story genres included here follows the recommended range of fiction text types for Years 1 and 2:

Y1T2: traditional stories;

Y1T2: fairy stories;

Y1T3: stories about fantasy worlds;

Y2T1: stories with familiar settings.

Within Text level work, there are a very large number of objectives relating to the reading and writing of the elements of stories, so they have not been listed here.

You may prefer to read the various story texts aloud to some groups of children, rather than expecting them to read them themselves.

The worksheets

The worksheets apply various strategies to demonstrate children's understanding of the different model texts: drawing out elements of the stories; sequencing the events; predicting what might happen after; role-playing characters; picking out particular vocabulary; changing the outcomes; drawing the shape of the plot.

Writing stories

Finally, specific help is given with planning the choices of character and plot, to encourage children's own writing in the model text types.

The Three Little Pigs (part 1)

A long time ago, three little pigs lived with their mother at the edge of the forest. One day their mother said, "Little pigs, you need to go into the forest and build your own homes."

So off went the three little pigs into the forest.

Before long, the biggest pig said, "Stop! I'm getting tired. I'll build my house here." And so he quickly built a small house out of straw. The other two pigs kept on walking.

Soon it was time for lunch, and the two little pigs stopped to have something to eat. "Brother," said the middle-sized pig, "I think I'll build my house right here." So he built a medium-sized house out of sticks and wood.

The last, smallest pig knew about the big bad wolf that lived in the forest so he built a big, strong house out of bricks.

One day the big bad wolf knocked on the door of the straw house. "Little pig, little pig, let me in, I'm hungry!" The biggest pig squeaked "No, no, I won't let you in." So the big bad wolf took a deep breath and blew the little straw house away.

The biggest pig ran as fast as he could to his brother's house of sticks. The big bad wolf knocked on the door. "Little pigs, little pigs, let me come in. I'm getting very hungry."

"No!" squealed the two little pigs. So the big bad wolf blew the stick house to pieces.

The Three Little Pigs (part 2)

The pigs ran to their little brother's brick house screaming "The big bad wolf is going to eat us for his dinner!"

The big bad wolf blew and blew, but he could not blow down the brick house. The big bad wolf climbed onto the roof of the house but the three little pigs built a huge fire in the fireplace. When the big bad wolf slid down the chimney, he fell into the fire. "Ouch!" he screamed.

The big bad wolf jumped back up the chimney
and ran away never to be seen again.
The three little pigs lived happily
ever after.

And all three lived in houses made
out of bricks, just in case.

When the pigs go visiting

Name _____

★ Draw the house you think the big bad wolf might have lived in.

★ What do you think might have happened if the pigs came to visit the wolf at his house? You might like to talk over your ideas with your partner.
Then write your ideas here.

_____

_____

_____

_____

_____

Sequencing

★ Cut out these pictures and put them in order to tell the story of 'The Three Little Pigs'. Then write a short caption underneath each picture to tell what happened.

Past tense

★ Stories can be written in the past tense. That means the story has already happened.

Read the story below. Put the words in brackets into the past tense. For example: get *(present)* / got *(past)*

A long time ago, three little pigs (live) _____

with their mother at the edge of the forest. One day

their mother (say) _____ , "Little pigs, you need

to go into the forest and build your own homes." So off

(go) _____ the three little pigs into the forest.

Before long, the biggest pig (shout) _____ "Stop!

I'm getting tired, I'll build my house here." And so he

quickly (build) _____ a small house out of straw.

The other two pigs (keep) _____ on walking.

Soon it (is) _____ time for lunch, and the two

little pigs (stop) _____ to have something to eat.

Diary entry

Name _____

★ Imagine you are the big bad wolf. Write your diary entry after you had been scared away by the three little pigs. Say why you visited the pigs' houses and how you felt when they tricked you.

_____

_____

_____

_____

_____

_____

_____

_____

_____

_____

_____

Innovation

Name _____

★ Work in a group to innovate, or change, the story 'The Three Little Pigs'.
Think about using different characters, changing what the characters did
and how the complication or problem could have been solved differently.

1. When will it happen?

_____

2. Where will it happen?

_____

3. Who are the characters?

_____

4. What will the complication(s) be?

_____

_____

_____

5. How will the problem(s) be solved?

_____

_____

_____

The Silly Wizard (part 1)

Once upon a time, deep in the forest, there lived a wizard named Elmo. Elmo had wanted to be a wizard ever since he was a little boy. He had practised and practised every day after school, doing card tricks and making a rabbit appear out of his hat. He always wore his pointy purple hat, even when he went to bed!

One day, Elmo decided to try his most daring trick, to turn his sister into a slimy green frog! This spell took a lot of preparation to get all the right ingredients. When he thought he was ready and the cauldron was boiling, Elmo called his sister, "Serena, Serena. I need your help."

"What is it now, Elmo? I'm busy feeding the animals," Serena called back from the shed.

"How am I going to be a great wizard when you won't help me?" Elmo said.

"Oh, all right," Serena agreed and she came out to see what Elmo wanted.

Elmo began to wave his wand over his head as he said:

"Toenail of an elephant,
Hair of a dog,
Bark of a tree,
Make Serena a frog!"

The Silly Wizard (part 2)

POOF! As the smoke disappeared, Serena was gone, and in her place was the ugliest, slimiest frog Elmo had ever seen. Yuck!

"Hooray!" shouted Elmo, "I'm the greatest wizard ever. Now all I have to do is turn her back again." But try as he might, Elmo could not reverse the spell. He tried this magic book and he tried that magic book, but nothing was working. What was he going to do?

Just then Elmo had an idea. "What if I say the spell backwards? It might work." It was a guess, but Elmo had to try something. He took a deep breath and said:

"Bark of a tree,
Hair of a dog,
Toenail of an elephant,
Serena is NOT a frog!"

POOF! Again there was a puff of smoke and Serena was standing where the slimy green frog had been. "Well, what did you want me for Elmo? I can't stand here for ever." "Oh, nothing," said Elmo, smiling. "I wonder what I can turn my little brother into?" he thought to himself.

Wizard words

Name _____

★ Read 'The Silly Wizard'. Draw a picture of Elmo, putting in as much detail as you can. Then write adjectives to describe him.

Elmo

Making a spell

Name _____

★ Work with a partner or in a group of three people.

Imagine you are wizards like Elmo. Make up a magic spell using some unusual ingredients. Try to make it rhyme!

This spell is for _____

The ingredients are _____

_____

_____

To make the spell work, say these words:

Hocus pocus

Name _____

★ Work with a partner to mime casting a spell.

To help you organise your mime, write down your ideas first.

Make sure you practise your mime before you show it to the rest of the class!

1. Who will be the wizard? _____

2. Who will have the spell put on them? _____

3. How will you mix the spell? _____

_____

4. Will you use a magic wand, or something else? _____

_____

5. What will you turn the person into? _____

_____

6. Do you need to use any props? If so, what will they be?

_____

_____

7. Use another sheet to draw yourself miming your spell.

Story path

Name _____

★ Every story has a special structure: setting the scene (called orientation), a complication (the problem) and a resolution (how the problem is solved).

Along the path through Elmo's forest, draw the main story parts from 'The Silly Wizard'. You could also write a short description of what happened at each stage of the story.

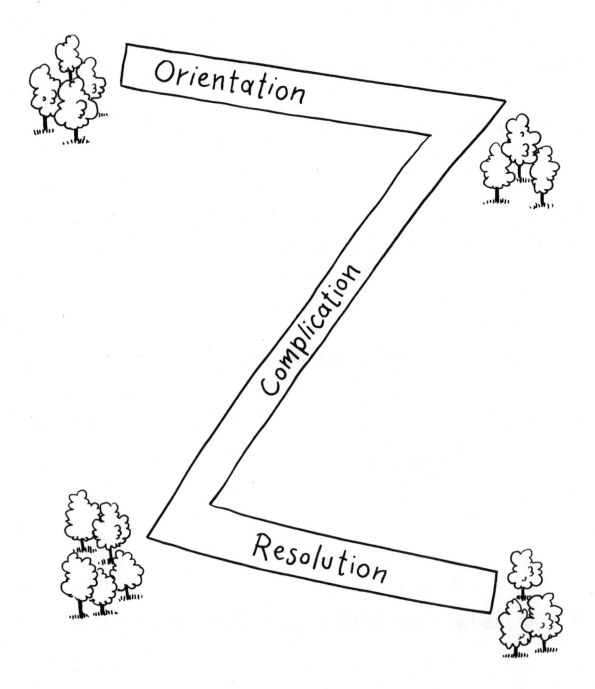

Interview a friend

Name _____

★ At the end of 'The Silly Wizard', Elmo begins to think about what magic spell he might put on his little brother.

Talk with a partner about what you think will happen next. Write down your ideas.

1. When do you think Elmo will try and put a spell on his brother?

_____

2. What do you think is the name of Elmo's brother?

_____

3. Will anyone help Elmo make this new spell? If so, who is it?

_____

_____

4. What ingredients will Elmo need for his new spell?

_____

_____

5. What might happen when Elmo tries this spell?

_____

_____

6. Will Elmo be able to reverse the spell put on his brother? If so, how will he do it?

_____

_____

The Lonely Spider (part 1)

A long time ago, there was a tiny little spider called Elanor, who lived all by herself. She was always very quiet. Nobody noticed her as she hid among the pretty flowers on the kitchen table.

Elanor liked her special home. But she was lonely! There was no-one to play with and no-one to talk to. How she wished there was something she could do.

Then one day, something terrible happened! The flowers in the vase were starting to die. Their leaves were drooping and the petals started to fall off. Suddenly a huge hand reached down, picked up the vase, carried it out of the door and down to the garden. Before Elanor knew it, she had been thrown out into the garden!

When she landed, Elanor shook herself dry. "Where am I?" she cried out to no-one in particular.

"You're in the garden, silly," a voice answered back.

"Who ... Who's that?" asked Elanor shyly.
"It's me. My name is Melvin. I'm a spider."

The Lonely Spider (part 2)

"I'm a spider too," said Elanor. "But I'm lonely and I don't have anywhere to go."

"You could come and play with me," said Melvin. "We could have lots of fun spinning webs together."

"Oh, could I? That would be great!" said Elanor, smiling.

So Elanor and Melvin found a lovely shady tree in the garden and began spinning their webs. Elanor had finally found a friend. And the two little spiders lived happily ever after.

Character profile

Name _____

★ In the box in the middle of the page, draw a picture of what you think the spiders look like. Then write some words to describe them (adjectives) in the shapes.

Create it

Name _____

★ Make Elanor's web and put her in it. You could use string, coloured paper, glue and other craft materials.

Sequencing

★ Here are some pictures from the story 'The Lonely Spider'. Cut them out. Then put them into the right order to tell the story.

Words that describe

Name _____

★ In the story 'The Lonely Spider' there are words that describe the characters and the setting (adjectives).

With your teacher, find them in the story and list some of them below.

_____   _____   _____

_____   _____   _____

_____   _____   _____

★ In the story there are also words that tell us what is happening. These words are doing words (verbs). They tell us what the characters did, felt or thought.

With your teacher, find the verbs in the story and list some of them below.

_____   _____   _____

_____   _____   _____

_____   _____   _____

From Time-Savers for Teachers: Writing Fiction Years 1-2. This page may be reproduced for classroom use.

75

Narrative structure

Name _____

★ In a small group, write about each picture to tell the story. Use the three stages of a narrative.

1. Orientation (the beginning of the story)

_____

_____

_____

_____

2. Complication (the problem in the story)

_____

_____

_____

_____

3. Resolution (the ending of the story)

_____

_____

_____

_____

Moving House (part 1)

It is Monday morning. Roger and his family are getting ready to move to the city. Roger doesn't want to go.

"Hurry up, Roger, the van is ready to go. We'll be late!" calls his mother.

"Oh all right," replies Roger, dragging his suitcase behind him. "But I still don't want to go. I know I'm going to hate it. The city is so noisy and smelly. Everyone rushes around and nobody listens to you."

"Don't worry so much," his mother tells him. "It'll be fun. Think of it as a new adventure."

"Mum, an adventure is wrestling wild crocodiles or flying to a distant planet in a spaceship. It is NOT moving to the city. I'll have no friends and there will be nothing to do."

The family finally arrive at their new home. It looks nice enough but poor Fitzroy, Roger's pet dog, is going to have to sleep in the laundry as his kennel won't fit in the garden.

The next day, Roger and his sister Jenny go with their mum to see their new school. Roger hates it already. The classrooms are grey and boring and the playground is made out of concrete. "Obviously they don't have a football team," he thinks to himself. "What a drag!"

"Smile, Mr Grumble," says Jenny. "It'll work out. Just give it some time."

"You sound like Mum," groans Roger. "What is there to smile about? I've got no friends, I can't play football on concrete, and all I want to do is go home."

Moving House (part 2)

Roger is in Year 3 and his new teacher's name is Mrs Goodman. "Good morning, Roger," she greets him warmly. "Welcome to 3G. There is a spare seat here next to Ben."

"Hello Roger, what do you like to do?" asks Ben.
"Well, I used to play football, but I can't do that here," Roger replies glumly.

"Oh don't worry about that," Ben tells him. "We've got monkey bars, and we're even allowed to climb trees. If you like, you can play with me at lunchtime."

Roger thinks about it for a minute. Climbing trees could be almost as much fun as football and hanging upside down on the monkey bars was something he used to do at his old school.

"That sounds good," he tells Ben. "I'll give you a race to the top of the monkey bars."

"You're on!" replies Ben, smiling.

Maybe living in the city isn't going to be so bad after all.

Role-play

Name _____

★ Get into groups of five. Each group member should take a role of one of the characters in the story. You can role-play the whole story, part of it, or even add your own ending when Ben and Roger play together at lunch-time. Remember to practise your roles. Make notes to help plan your ideas.

Character:	_____ _____
_____	
Character:	_____ _____
_____	
Character:	_____ _____
_____	
Character:	_____ _____
_____	
Character:	_____ _____
_____	
We will need (props):	

Positive and negative

Name _____

★ Think about the positive (good) things that might happen to Roger now that he has moved house. List them.

Then list all the negative (bad) things that Roger might not like about moving house. You could use your own experiences to help you, or talk about it with a partner.

POSITIVE (GOOD)	NEGATIVE (BAD)

Narrative structure

Name _____

★ Answer the following questions to describe what happened in each stage of 'Moving House'.

ORIENTATION

When did it happen? _____

Where did it happen? _____

Who are the main characters? _____

COMPLICATION

What did Roger think was the problem with moving house? (There may be more than one.)

_____

_____

_____

RESOLUTION

How were Roger's problems resolved? _____

_____

Who helped him solve them? _____

What did Roger do once his problems were solved? _____

_____

Talk to a friend

Name _____

★ Work with a partner. Ask him/her whether they have ever had to do something that they didn't want to do.

My friend's name _____

1. When did it happen? _____

2. Where did it happen? _____

3. What went wrong? (There may be more than one event.)

_____

_____

4. Who solved the problem? _____

_____

5. How was the problem solved? _____

_____

_____

6. What happened after the problem was solved? _____

_____

_____

Research

Name _____

★ You and your family are moving. You may choose to move to another country or to another city. Choose a place that you would like to go to and find out some facts about it. Write about its best features and why you would like to move there. Remember to include pictures, diagrams and maps to support your ideas.

You can work by yourself, with a partner or in a small group.

Narrative choices

Name _____

★   Circle an idea, or write your own to plan your own narrative.

Orientation
WHEN?

a long time ago   last week   _____

WHERE?

in a gloomy cave   at school   in my garden

on another planet   in a castle   _____

WHO? (can be more than one)

wizard   fairy   witch   alien   monster   ghost

teacher   friend   animal   princess   prince   _____

Complication
WHAT?

taken to another planet   turned into an animal

scared by a ghost   had an accident

got lost   forgot to do homework

didn't have any friends   _____

Resolution
HOW?

was helped by someone   used a magic spell

didn't come back   made a friend

was granted a wish   _____

Ending

lived happily ever after   never came back again

they never did it again   it was the happiest time

what would happen tomorrow?   _____

Narrative outline

Name _____

Orientation

When? _____

_____

Where? _____

_____

Who? _____

_____

Complication (or problem)

_____

_____

_____

Resolution (solving the problem)

_____

_____

_____

Ending

_____

_____

Narrative skills checklist

Name:				
Class:	Date/Level	Date/Level	Date/Level	Date/Level
PURPOSE				
Understands the purpose of a narrative – to tell a story.				
STRUCTURE				
Decides upon an appropriate title.				
Identifies the three main stages.				
Locates the orientation, complication and resolution in a known narrative.				
Suggests relevant complications.				
Suggests relevant resolutions.				
TEXT ORGANISATION				
Correctly sequences events.				
Retells a familiar narrative.				
Records events from familiar narratives.				
Jointly constructs a narrative.				
Uses a scaffold to write own narrative.				
Creates a story map.				
Writes an orientation.				
Lists possible topics for a narrative.				
LANGUAGE FEATURES				
Uses simple past tense.				
Correctly uses conjunctions.				
Uses simple time connectives.				
Uses action verbs.				
Uses adjectives to describe nouns and noun groups.				
Uses capitals and full stops.				
Attempts to use dialogue.				
Uses third person correctly.				
Begins to separate stages by using paragraphs.				
Begins sentences in different ways.				

LEVEL CODES   1 Consistently evident   2 Sometimes evident   3 Not evident

Introduction to Writing about fiction

NLS objectives

Although some review writing could be classified as non-fiction, under headings of e.g. persuasive or informative text, we include it here because the personal response to fiction follows so immediately from children's reading of fiction.

The text level objectives do specify the development of personal responses to fiction, with justified reasoning:

Y1T3 T10: to compare and contrast preferences and common themes in stories and poems;

Y2T3 T12: to write simple evaluations of books read and discussed, giving reasons.

The worksheets

After one model review of a picture-book text, children are given frameworks and scaffolds to use on any text of their choice.

They are encouraged to consider the separate elements of character, illustration and plot, before considering their own personal opinion; and finally, it is suggested that children conduct a whole-class survey on their favourite author.

I read 'Willy the Wimp'

I read the book 'Willy the Wimp' by Anthony Browne. He also illustrated it.

In the story Willy is a worrier. Everybody thinks he is weak.

One day he reads about how to be strong. He tries lots of ways to become strong, like body-building and aerobics.

Then he saves his friend from the gorilla bullies and feels very proud of himself and very strong.

This book is really funny because the pictures show how Willy really feels as he tries different things.

Describe a character

Name _____

The main character of this story is _____

★ Write a word to describe each feature.

Appearance:

Hair _____

Eyes _____

Size _____

Approximate age _____

★ Write two or more words to describe the character's personality.

_____

★ Draw a picture showing how you think the character looks.

Story plot

Name _____

The book is called _____

The main character is _____

First, _____

_____

_____

Then, _____

_____

_____

Next, _____

_____

_____

In the end, _____

_____

_____

Plan a response

Before you begin, think about:

Who will read this response? (Who is the audience?)

Why would they read it? (What is its purpose?)

What to do

1. Write down the full title, and the author and illustrator.

2. Give some details of what happened in the story.

3. Decide what you think and how you feel about the story. Give your opinion of it.

Editing and checking

Ask yourself:

Have I put in enough detail?

Have I stated my opinion clearly?

Thinking notes

Name _____

★ Use this page to make notes on some of the things you will include in your response.

Title _____

1. Who wrote this book? _____

2. Who are the main characters? _____

_____

3. Which character is your favourite and why? _____

_____

4. What do you like about the story? What don't you like?

_____

_____

5. How would you change the story if you were the author?

_____

_____

6. What do you think of the illustrations?

_____

_____

My response

Name _____

My book is called _____

It is by _____

I like it because _____

_____

_____

_____

_____

Response scaffold

Name _____

Title, author, illustrator of the text:

_____

_____

_____

_____

Sequence of events in the story:

_____

_____

_____

_____

My opinion:

_____

_____

_____

_____

Survey form

Name _____

★ Use this page to find out who is the favourite author of the friends in your class.

Name	Name of favourite author

Number of people in survey _____

The author most people liked was _____

Number of people who liked that author _____

Response skills checklist

Name:				
Class:	Date/Level	Date/Level	Date/Level	Date/Level
PURPOSE				
Understands that a response contains personal opinion of a text.				
Knows that responses give information about texts.				
STRUCTURE				
Understands that responses begin with a statement about title, author and illustrator.				
Knows that an opinion is usually given at the end.				
ORGANISATION				
Knows that responses contain details of title, author and illustrator.				
Knows that responses usually give detail of plot.				
Knows that responses contain an opinion, usually at the end.				
LANGUAGE FEATURES				
Uses thinking and relating verbs.				
Uses present tense.				
Attempts to summarise plot using temporal sequence.				
Attempts to state opinion using persuasive language.				
LEVEL CODES 1 Consistently evident		2 Sometimes evident		3 Not evident